21st Century
Junior Library

INFOGRAPHICS:
INCENTIVES

Christina Hill

Econo-Graphics Jr.

Published in the United States of America by:

CHERRY LAKE PUBLISHING GROUP
Ann Arbor, Michigan
www.cherrylakepublishing.com

Reading Adviser: Beth Walker Gambro, MS, Ed., Reading Consultant, Yorkville, IL
Photo Credits: © Cover, Page 1: ©elena/Getty Images; Page 5: ©Sylfida/Shutterstock, ©iKandy/ Shutterstock; Page 7: ©OpenClipart-Vectors/ Pixabay; Page 10: ©Artisticco/Shutterstock; Page 11: ©Boy Odachi/Shutterstock; Page 15: ©United States Environmental Protection Agency/ Wikimedia, ©Andrew19/Shutterstock, ©Vector Tradition/Shutterstock, ©Irina Strelnikova/Shutterstock; Page 17: ©Memed_Nurrohmad/Pixaba Page 19: ©SurfsUp/Shutterstock; Page 20: ©OpenClipart-Vectors/Pixabay, ©Sergii Korolko/Shutterstock, © Bens-Photos/Shutterstock; Page 2 ©Benefphic/Shutterstock; Page 22: ©Bonezboyz/Shutterstock

Cherry Lake Press is an imprint of Cherry Lake Publishing Group.

Library of Congress Cataloging-in-Publication Data
Names: Hill, Christina, author.
Title: Infographics. Incentives / Christina Hill.
Other titles: Incentives
Description: Ann Arbor, Michigan : Cherry Lake Publishing, [2023] | Series: Econo-graphics Jr. | Includes bibliographical references and index. |
    Audience: Grades 2-3 | Summary: "How do incentives work? In the Econo-Graphics Jr. series, young readers will examine economy-related
    issues from many angles, all portrayed through visual elements. Income, budgeting, investing, supply and demand, global markets, inflation,
    and more are covered. Each book highlights pandemic-era impacts as well. Created with developing readers in mind, charts, graphs, maps, an
    infographics provide key content in an engaging and accessible way. Books include an activity, glossary, index, suggested reading and website
    and a bibliography"— Provided by publisher.
Identifiers: LCCN 2022037921 | ISBN 9781668919279 (hardcover) | ISBN 9781668920299 (paperback) | ISBN 9781668921623 (ebook) |
    ISBN 9781668922958 (pdf)
Subjects: LCSH: Tax incentives—Juvenile literature. | Subsidies—Juvenile literature. | Economics—Juvenile literature.
Classification: LCC HJ2330 .H65 2023 | DDC 336.24/316—dc23/eng/20220906
LC record available at https://lccn.loc.gov/2022037921
Cherry Lake Publishing Group would like to acknowledge the work of the Partnership for 21st Century Learning, a network of Battelle for Kids.
Please visit http://www.battelleforkids.org/networks/p21 for more information.

Printed in the United States of America
Corporate Graphics

Before embracing a career as an author, **Christina Hill** received a bachelor's degree in English from the University of California, Irvine, and a graduate degree in literature from California State University, Long Beach. When she is not writing about various subjects from sports to economics, Christina can be found hiking, mastering yoga handstands, or curled up with a classic novel. Christina lives in sunny Southern Californ with her husband, two sons, and beloved dog, Pepper Riley.

CONTENTS

WHAT ARE INCENTIVES?

Positive and negative **incentives** push people to do things. Some incentives push people to do things that make them feel good. Some incentives involve money. Most of those incentives push people to do things for a reward or to avoid punishment.

Workplace Incentives

Positive Incentive
Workers can receive a bonus if they make a certain number of parts.

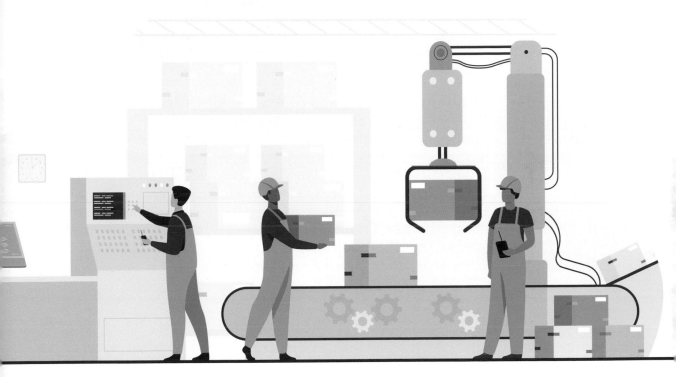

Negative Incentive
Workers may not receive the bonus if they make faulty or broken parts.

Timeline of Cereal Box Incentives

1909	Kellogg's Corn Flakes offers a mail-order storybook with the purchase of two boxes. More than 2.5 million people request the offer.
1945	Kellogg's adds a pin-backed button to their cereal boxes. It is the first inside-the-box prize.
1969	Super Sugar Crisps cereal offers a four-song cut-out record on the back of the box. (It actually plays!)
1979	Cheerios offers mail-order dartboards.
1981	Cocoa Puffs offers free bubble gum inside its cereal boxes.
1990	Jetsons cereal boxes offer a plastic lunar launcher toy.
2015	Cinnamon Toast Crunch offers droid viewers that include a sneak peek of the latest *Star Wars* movie.
2018	Froot Loops offers a chance to win free movie tickets.

TAX INCENTIVES

Governments give people **tax** incentives. If people buy or do certain things, the government lowers the taxes they pay.

Top 10 U.S. States with Solar Tax Incentives (2021)

Solar energy is more Earth-friendly than fossil fuels such as coal. Solar tax incentives give people extra reasons to "go green."

Some states offer homeowners with solar the choice to deduct 25% of their solar energy expense from their taxes.

7. Colorado

6. New Mexico

2022, Energy.gov

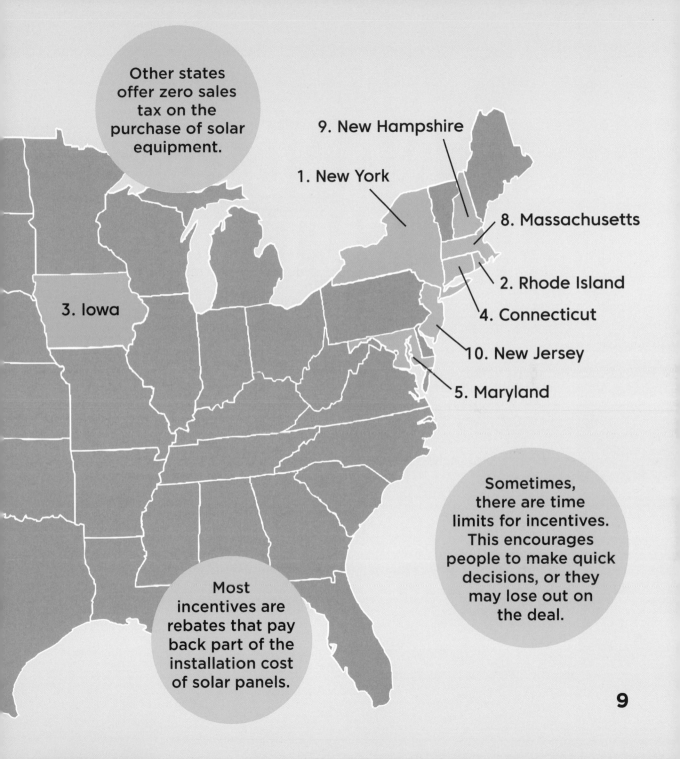

Other states offer zero sales tax on the purchase of solar equipment.

9. New Hampshire

1. New York

8. Massachusetts

2. Rhode Island

4. Connecticut

10. New Jersey

5. Maryland

3. Iowa

Sometimes, there are time limits for incentives. This encourages people to make quick decisions, or they may lose out on the deal.

Most incentives are rebates that pay back part of the installation cost of solar panels.

FINANCIAL INCENTIVES

Many companies offer **financial** incentives. These may be punch cards to earn a free item. Or they could be special prices for store members. This is how Costco works.

Businesses also offer financial incentives to their workers. They give them raises and bonuses.

Costco Memberships on the Rise (2014–2020)

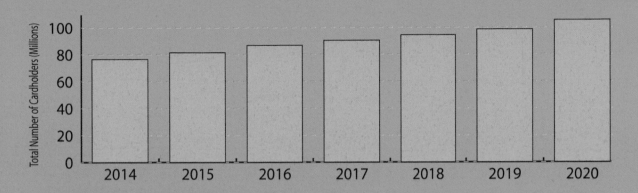

Total Number of Cardholders (Millions)

2022, Statista: 2022, Costco

Starbucks Rewards Program

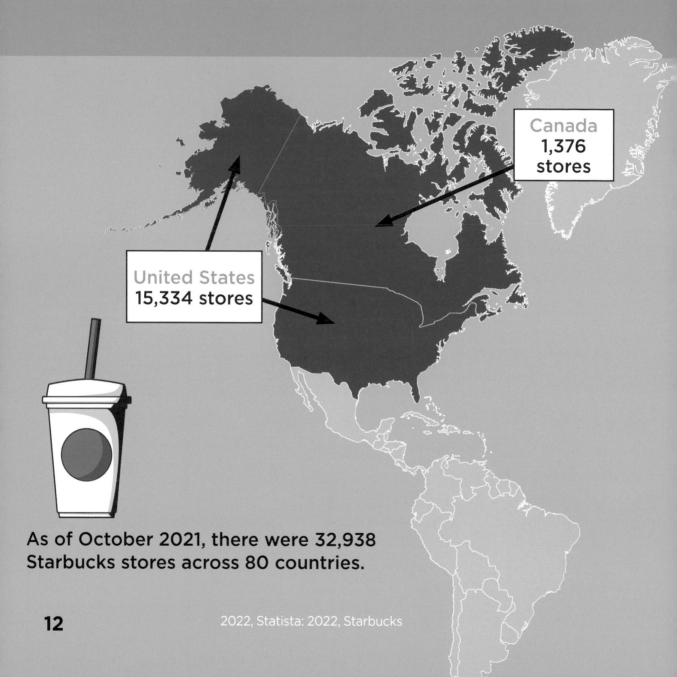

Canada
**1,376
stores**

United States
15,334 stores

As of October 2021, there were 32,938
Starbucks stores across 80 countries.

2022, Statista: 2022, Starbucks

and Customer Loyalty

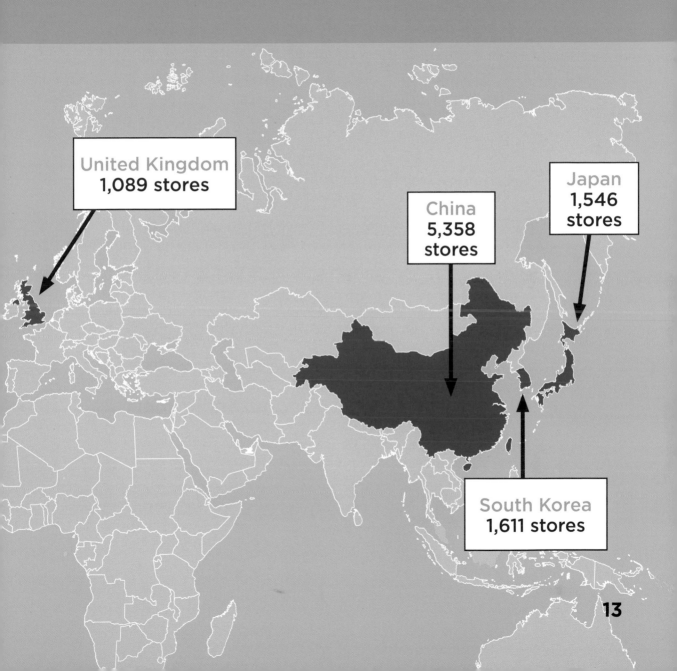

United Kingdom
1,089 stores

China
**5,358
stores**

Japan
**1,546
stores**

South Korea
1,611 stores

SUBSIDIES

A **subsidy** is money that a government gives businesses. This money helps protect jobs and keep prices down. Subsidies can also help people. **Public assistance** and **unemployment** benefits are subsidies.

Where Do U.S. Public Assistance Dollars Go?

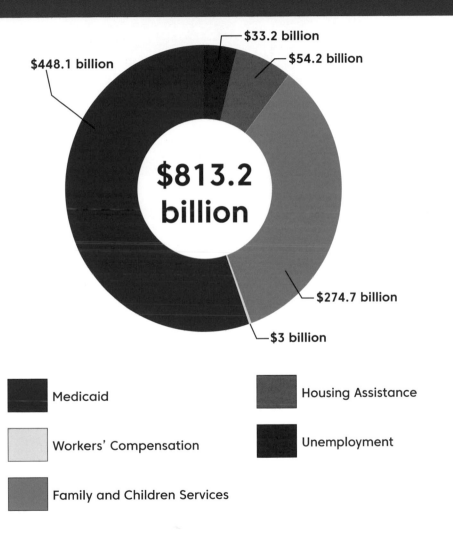

$33.2 billion

$54.2 billion

$448.1 billion

$813.2 billion

$274.7 billion

$3 billion

Medicaid

Housing Assistance

Workers' Compensation

Unemployment

Family and Children Services

2021, U.S.Government Spending

15

Energy Star Savings

ENERGY STAR is a U.S. government program. It is run by the Environmental Protection Agency (EPA) and the Department of Energy (DOE).

It gives incentives to people who buy energy-saving appliances. They get money back from the program.

Every dollar the EPA spends on ENERGY STAR results in $350 in savings for businesses and homes.

In 2019, Americans saved $39 billion in energy costs by using ENERGY STAR appliances.

2020, ENERGY STAR

Electric Car Subsidies

Since 2010, the U.S. government offers some **consumers** who buy electric cars a $7,500 tax credit.

In 2010, Tesla received a $465 million loan from the U.S. DOE to make more fuel-efficient cars.

The United Kingdom offers a $2,900 discount for new electric cars.

In Norway, electric car drivers can pay less in taxes and parking costs.

The Cost of College

The U.S. government offers **subsidized** student loans for college students. These loans save students money. The government pays the **interest** on the loans while students attend school.

Subsidized % VS Unsubsidized %

Fast Facts

- The average cost of college in the United States is $35,720 per year.
- The average amount owed on a student loan is $39,351.
- Each year, about one-third of college students borrow money.
- The average student borrows more than $30,000.

2021, Education Data Initiative

NEGATIVE INCENTIVES

Not all incentives are positive ones. Negative incentives can also push people to do things. If you are often late to school, you might get detention. Drivers who speed may get a ticket.

The Price of Breaking the Law

About 112,000 U.S. drivers get speeding tickets each day.

The average speeding ticket costs $150.

The state with the most speeding tickets in 2021 was Ohio. Sixteen percent of its drivers got a ticket

Each year, 41 million U.S. drivers receive a speeding ticket.

The government collects $6.23 billion each year from speeding tickets.

2021, Insurify; 2021 Hamilton & Associates

Plastic Bans and Fees

Some U.S. states have banned single-use plastic bags.

In other states, stores must charge consumers for plastic bags. Many charge 10 cents per bag.

Of the 50 U.S. states, 26 have plastics bans in place.

San Jose, California has a plastic bag fee. Its bag litter in creeks and rivers is down 76%. Park and roadside bag litter is down 59%. Bag litter in storm drains is down 69%.

ACTIVITY
A Week of Incentives

Menu

- Tacos $2.00
- Chips and Salsa $1.50
- Rice and Beans $2.00
- Soda $1.00
- Churro $1.50

Your older brother bought a taco truck. He wants more business. He wants to use incentives.

Help your brother create five financial incentives. These incentives should encourage customers to buy more food and drinks. See the chapter on financial incentives for ideas.

Create an advertising poster that lists the five incentive options.